I AM WHAT A FEMINIST LOOKS LIKE

Created, published, and distributed by Knock Knock
6080 Center Drive
Los Angeles, CA 90045
knockknockstuff.com
Knock Knock is a registered trademark of Knock Knock LLC
Inner-Truth is a registered trademark of Knock Knock LLC

This book is meant solely for entertainment purposes. In no event will
Knock Knock be liable to any reader for any harm, injury, or damages,
including direct, indirect, incidental, special, consequential, or punitive
arising out of or in connection with the use of the information contained
in this book. So there.

ISBN: 978-168349166-8
UPC: 825703-50168-1

10 9 8 7 6 5 4 3 2 1

SO WAIT, WHAT DOES A FEMINIST REALLY LOOK LIKE?

WELL, PERHAPS YOU HAVE HEARD SOMETHING ALONG THESE (UNFLATTERING, UN-FUN, "UN-WOKE") LINES ONCE OR TWICE OR A MILLION times before: angry, uppity, bra-burning, humorless, hairy, homely, aggressive, witchy, bitchy, man-hating.

Luckily, you know better. YOU know what a feminist looks like. A feminist looks like your best friend, the guy who served you that latte, Gloria Steinem, the cute four-year-old in her soccer cleats, the Dalai Lama, your grandmother. A feminist looks like you.

Webster frames feminism this way:
1: the theory of the political, economic, and social equality of the sexes
2: organized activity on behalf of women's rights and interests

A T-shirt designed by Cheris Kramarae and Paula Treichler gets more to the point: "Feminism is the radical idea that women are people too." Bingo.

There are so many feminist role models to help you nurture your feminist identity. We tend to think of recent heroes like Malala Yousafzai, Ruth Bader Ginsburg, Emma Watson, and John Legend. Or we look to the feminist icons of a previous generation, like Gloria Steinem, bell hooks, and Angela Davis. Or even the OG variety of suffragettes like Susan B. Anthony, Elizabeth Cady Stanton, and Emmeline Pankhurst.

But while the term "feminism" was first used in 1841, feminist mavericks existed long before that. They'll also show you what a feminist looks like.

There are leaders like Nzinga Mbandi, seventeenth-century Queen of Ndongo and Matamba (now Angola) who was a brilliant diplomat, politician, and warrior, and Queen Elizabeth I of Great Britain, who remained unmarried rather than cede power to a potential husband.

How about a badass like Qutulun, a thirteenth-century Mongolian warrior princess, who swore to only marry a man who could beat her at wrestling? Those who failed had to gift her with horses. Story has it, she built up quite a stable. Or Æthelflæd, Lady of the Mercians, a tenth-century Anglo-Saxon warrior queen who protected her country (in current England) from repeated Viking attacks?

You could also look to the seventeenth-century Mexican poet, Sor Juana Inés de la Cruz, who wrote pretty racy stuff, spoke out against misogyny, and became a nun in order to continue her work. Check out Murasaki Shikibu of Japan, who wrote *The Tale of Genji*—the world's first novel—in the early eleventh century. She learned Chinese by listening to her brothers' lessons through the door, since she wasn't allowed to study herself.

You can model your strength on Sojourner Truth, who escaped slavery, was outspoken on women's rights, and who was the first black woman to win a court case against a white man. You could be as accomplished as German Hildegard von Bingen, who lived in the 1100s and advised kings and popes, composed music and poetry, and wrote on science, medicine, and philosophy. You could be as daring as Artemisia Gentileschi, a celebrated Italian Baroque artist, best known for the rather bloody painting *Judith Slaying Holofernes*.

While we're looking at history, let's give a nod to some excellent men who advocated for women's equality, like abolitionist Frederick Douglass, English philosopher and economist John Stuart Mill, and the first president of Turkey, Mustafa Kemal Atatürk.

So how do you nurture your feminist identity other than diving into feminist history? How do you grow, learn, and make sure you're holding to your values? You could write about it in a journal! Journaling can help you become the feminist—and the person—you want to be.

As noted self-help guru Deepak Chopra claims, "Journaling is one of the most powerful tools we have to transform our lives." According to a widely- cited study by James W. Pennebaker and Janel D. Seagal, "Writing about important personal experiences in an emotional way . . . brings about improvements in mental and physical health." Proven benefits include better stress management, strengthened immune systems, fewer doctor visits, and improvement in chronic illnesses such as asthma.

It's not entirely clear how journaling accomplishes all this. Catharsis is involved, but many also point to the value of organizing experiences into a cohesive narrative. According to *Newsweek*, some experts believe that journaling "forces us to transform the ruminations cluttering our minds into coherent stories."

What should you write about? Practice being your own best, empowered self and celebrate that. Write about the misogyny you see and how you can counter it. Practice spelling "misogyny." Write about the feminists you admire. Write when you see evidence of increased equality. Write to renew yourself after you make the mistake of reading online comments. Write whatever comes, and don't criticize it; journaling is a means of self-reflection, not a structured composition. In other words, be free, be human, liberate your inner warrior/goddess/mermaid—and just DO YOU on the page. If you find yourself unable to think of anything to write, don't stress. Instead, use the quotes inside this journal as a jumping-off point for observations and explorations.

Finally, determine a home for your journal where you can find it easily. Perhaps keep it near your copies of *The Handmaid's Tale, Bad Feminist,* and *The Feminine Mystique.*

In an inspiring speech on confidence, comedian and actor Amy Schumer said, "I say if I'm beautiful. I say if I'm strong. You will not determine my story—I will." You could easily add to that, "I say if I'm a feminist." No one but you can determine what kind of feminist you are, no one can tell you you're doing it right or wrong. You are what a feminist looks like, thinks like, and acts like, and you get to decide what that means. Have at it, grrrl (or however you identify)!

I am no bird; and
no net ensnares me;
I am a free human
being with an
independent will.

JANE EYRE *(JANE EYRE)*

HOW I'M MAKING MY VOICE HEARD TODAY:

_____

_____

_____

_____

_____

_____

_____

_____

_____

_____

_____

_____

_____

_____

_____

_____

_____

_____

_____

_____

_____

_____

_____

TODAY'S PERSONAL-EMPOWERMENT LEVEL:

We liked to be known as the clever girls. When we decorated our hands with henna for holidays and weddings, we drew calculus and chemical formulae instead of flowers and butterflies.

MALALA YOUSAFZAI

DATE		

HOW I'M MAKING MY VOICE HEARD TODAY:

_____

_____

_____

_____

_____

_____

_____

_____

_____

_____

_____

_____

_____

_____

_____

_____

_____

_____

_____

_____

_____

_____

TODAY'S PERSONAL-EMPOWERMENT LEVEL:

Even in space, there's a double standard.

CARRIE FISHER

DATE		

HOW I'M MAKING MY VOICE HEARD TODAY:

_____

_____

_____

_____

_____

_____

_____

_____

_____

_____

_____

_____

_____

_____

_____

_____

_____

_____

_____

_____

_____

_____

TODAY'S PERSONAL-EMPOWERMENT LEVEL:

I myself have never been able to find out precisely what feminism is: I only know that people call me a feminist whenever I express sentiments that differentiate me from a doormat.

REBECCA WEST

HOW I'M MAKING MY VOICE HEARD TODAY:

_____

_____

_____

_____

_____

_____

_____

_____

_____

_____

_____

_____

_____

_____

_____

_____

_____

_____

_____

_____

_____

_____

_____

TODAY'S PERSONAL-EMPOWERMENT LEVEL:

I would have girls regard themselves not as adjectives but nouns.

ELIZABETH CADY STANTON

HOW I'M MAKING MY VOICE HEARD TODAY:

_____

_____

_____

_____

_____

_____

_____

_____

_____

_____

_____

_____

_____

_____

_____

_____

_____

_____

_____

_____

_____

_____

_____

TODAY'S PERSONAL-EMPOWERMENT LEVEL:

The last thing I wanted was infinite security and to be the place an arrow shoots off from. I wanted change and excitement and to shoot off in all directions myself, like the colored arrows from a Fourth of July rocket.

SYLVIA PLATH

HOW I'M MAKING MY VOICE HEARD TODAY:

_____

_____

_____

_____

_____

_____

_____

_____

_____

_____

_____

_____

_____

_____

_____

_____

_____

_____

_____

_____

_____

_____

_____

_____

TODAY'S PERSONAL-EMPOWERMENT LEVEL:

I don't want to make somebody else. I want to make myself.

TONI MORRISON

HOW I'M MAKING MY VOICE HEARD TODAY:

_____
_____
_____
_____
_____
_____
_____
_____
_____
_____
_____
_____
_____
_____
_____
_____
_____
_____
_____
_____
_____
_____
_____
_____
_____

TODAY'S PERSONAL-EMPOWERMENT LEVEL:

Equality is like gravity. We need it to stand on this earth as men and women, and the misogyny that is in every culture is not a true part of the human condition.

JOSS WHEDON

HOW I'M MAKING MY VOICE HEARD TODAY:

_____

_____

_____

_____

_____

_____

_____

_____

_____

_____

_____

_____

_____

_____

_____

_____

_____

_____

_____

_____

_____

_____

_____

_____

_____

_____

TODAY'S PERSONAL-EMPOWERMENT LEVEL:

Here she comes, running, out of prison and off pedestal; chains off, crown off, halo off, just a live woman.

CHARLOTTE PERKINS GILMAN

DATE		

HOW I'M MAKING MY VOICE HEARD TODAY:

_____

_____

_____

_____

_____

_____

_____

_____

_____

_____

_____

_____

_____

_____

_____

_____

_____

_____

_____

_____

_____

TODAY'S PERSONAL-EMPOWERMENT LEVEL:

If you want to be real tough, you should grow a vagina. Those things can take a pounding.

SHENG WANG

DATE		

HOW I'M MAKING MY VOICE HEARD TODAY:

_____

_____

_____

_____

_____

_____

_____

_____

_____

_____

_____

_____

_____

_____

_____

_____

_____

_____

_____

_____

_____

_____

TODAY'S PERSONAL-EMPOWERMENT LEVEL:

Above all, be the heroine of your life,
not the victim.

NORA EPHRON

HOW I'M MAKING MY VOICE HEARD TODAY:

_____

_____

_____

_____

_____

_____

_____

_____

_____

_____

_____

_____

_____

_____

_____

_____

_____

_____

_____

_____

_____

_____

TODAY'S PERSONAL-EMPOWERMENT LEVEL:

Some people say I'm an overachiever, but I think they're just jealous.

TRACY FLICK *(ELECTION)*

DATE

HOW I'M MAKING MY VOICE HEARD TODAY:

_____
_____
_____
_____
_____
_____
_____
_____
_____
_____
_____
_____
_____
_____
_____
_____
_____
_____
_____
_____
_____
_____
_____
_____

TODAY'S PERSONAL-EMPOWERMENT LEVEL:

Well-behaved women seldom make history.

LAUREL THATCHER ULRICH

DATE

HOW I'M MAKING MY VOICE HEARD TODAY:

_____

_____

_____

_____

_____

_____

_____

_____

_____

_____

_____

_____

_____

_____

_____

_____

_____

_____

_____

_____

_____

TODAY'S PERSONAL-EMPOWERMENT LEVEL:

As soon as a woman gets to an age
where she has opinions and she's vital
and she's strong, she's systematically
shamed into hiding under a rock.

SARAH SILVERMAN

DATE

HOW I'M MAKING MY VOICE HEARD TODAY:

I have been broken, so
I am prepared should
that happen again....
You have no idea
what I can take.

———————
ROXANE GAY

HOW I'M MAKING MY VOICE HEARD TODAY:

_____

_____

_____

_____

_____

_____

_____

_____

_____

_____

_____

_____

_____

_____

_____

_____

_____

_____

_____

_____

_____

_____

_____

TODAY'S PERSONAL-EMPOWERMENT LEVEL:

Time's up on the female condition.
Gender equality can't just exist outside
ourselves—it must exist within.
We must take responsibility not just
for our actions, but for ourselves.

SCARLETT JOHANSSON

HOW I'M MAKING MY VOICE HEARD TODAY:

_____
_____
_____
_____
_____
_____
_____
_____
_____
_____
_____
_____
_____
_____
_____
_____
_____
_____
_____
_____
_____
_____
_____
_____
_____

TODAY'S PERSONAL-EMPOWERMENT LEVEL:

I'm not the next Usain Bolt or Michael Phelps. I'm the first Simone Biles.

SIMONE BILES

HOW I'M MAKING MY VOICE HEARD TODAY:

_____

_____

_____

_____

_____

_____

_____

_____

_____

_____

_____

_____

_____

_____

_____

_____

_____

_____

_____

_____

_____

_____

TODAY'S PERSONAL-EMPOWERMENT LEVEL:

I do not wish [women]
to have power over men;
but over themselves.

MARY WOLLSTONECRAFT

DATE

HOW I'M MAKING MY VOICE HEARD TODAY:

_____

_____

_____

_____

_____

_____

_____

_____

_____

_____

_____

_____

_____

_____

_____

_____

_____

_____

_____

_____

_____

_____

_____

_____

TODAY'S PERSONAL-EMPOWERMENT LEVEL:

I believe in the resistance as I believe there can be no light without shadow; or rather, no shadow unless there is also light.

———————

OFFRED *(THE HANDMAID'S TALE)*

HOW I'M MAKING MY VOICE HEARD TODAY:

_____

_____

_____

_____

_____

_____

_____

_____

_____

_____

_____

_____

_____

_____

_____

_____

_____

_____

_____

_____

_____

_____

_____

_____

_____

TODAY'S PERSONAL-EMPOWERMENT LEVEL:

In the future, there will be no female leaders. There will just be leaders.

SHERYL SANDBERG

HOW I'M MAKING MY VOICE HEARD TODAY:

_____

_____

_____

_____

_____

_____

_____

_____

_____

_____

_____

_____

_____

_____

_____

_____

_____

_____

_____

_____

_____

TODAY'S PERSONAL-EMPOWERMENT LEVEL:

I know that, like every woman of the people, I have more strength than I appear to have.

——————

EVA PERÓN

HOW I'M MAKING MY VOICE HEARD TODAY:

_____

_____

_____

_____

_____

_____

_____

_____

_____

_____

_____

_____

_____

_____

_____

_____

_____

_____

_____

_____

_____

_____

_____

_____

TODAY'S PERSONAL-EMPOWERMENT LEVEL:

How could it be any more obvious that we still live in a patriarchal world when feminism is a bad word?

ELLEN PAGE

HOW I'M MAKING MY VOICE HEARD TODAY:

_____

_____

_____

_____

_____

_____

_____

_____

_____

_____

_____

_____

_____

_____

_____

_____

_____

_____

_____

_____

_____

_____

_____

_____

_____

_____

_____

_____

TODAY'S PERSONAL-EMPOWERMENT LEVEL:

I don't like to smile unless I have a reason.

DARIA *(DARIA)*

HOW I'M MAKING MY VOICE HEARD TODAY:

_____

_____

_____

_____

_____

_____

_____

_____

_____

_____

_____

_____

_____

_____

_____

_____

_____

_____

_____

_____

_____

_____

_____

TODAY'S PERSONAL-EMPOWERMENT LEVEL:

It's important to have female characters. It's wonderful for women to mentor other women, but it's just as important for women to mentor men and vice-versa.

MINDY KALING

DATE	

HOW I'M MAKING MY VOICE HEARD TODAY:

_____
_____
_____
_____
_____
_____
_____
_____
_____
_____
_____
_____
_____
_____
_____
_____
_____
_____
_____
_____
_____
_____
_____

TODAY'S PERSONAL-EMPOWERMENT LEVEL:

A lot of people seem to think that feminism is against men, or pits women against men, which is not my perception of it and not what my mom taught me at all.

JOSEPH GORDON-LEVITT

DATE

HOW I'M MAKING MY VOICE HEARD TODAY:

_____
_____
_____
_____
_____
_____
_____
_____
_____
_____
_____
_____
_____
_____
_____
_____
_____
_____
_____
_____
_____
_____
_____
_____

TODAY'S PERSONAL-EMPOWERMENT LEVEL:

Here's to no ceiling at all!

MINNIE DRIVER

HOW I'M MAKING MY VOICE HEARD TODAY:

_____

_____

_____

_____

_____

_____

_____

_____

_____

_____

_____

_____

_____

_____

_____

_____

_____

_____

_____

_____

_____

_____

_____

TODAY'S PERSONAL-EMPOWERMENT LEVEL:

You are built not
to shrink down to
less, but to blossom
into more.

OPRAH WINFREY

DATE	

HOW I'M MAKING MY VOICE HEARD TODAY:

_____

_____

_____

_____

_____

_____

_____

_____

_____

_____

_____

_____

_____

_____

_____

_____

_____

_____

_____

_____

_____

_____

_____

TODAY'S PERSONAL-EMPOWERMENT LEVEL:

Women have served all these centuries as looking-glasses possessing the magic and delicious power of reflecting the figure of man at twice its natural size.

VIRGINIA WOOLF

DATE		

HOW I'M MAKING MY VOICE HEARD TODAY:

_____

_____

_____

_____

_____

_____

_____

_____

_____

_____

_____

_____

_____

_____

_____

_____

_____

_____

_____

_____

_____

_____

_____

TODAY'S PERSONAL-EMPOWERMENT LEVEL:

I don't want to cover up anymore. Not my face, not my mind, not my soul, not my thoughts, not my dreams, not my struggles, not my emotional growth. Nothing.

ALICIA KEYS

HOW I'M MAKING MY VOICE HEARD TODAY:

TODAY'S PERSONAL-EMPOWERMENT LEVEL:

Being powerful is so much more interesting than being beautiful.

HELEN MIRREN

DATE

HOW I'M MAKING MY VOICE HEARD TODAY:

_____

_____

_____

_____

_____

_____

_____

_____

_____

_____

_____

_____

_____

_____

_____

_____

_____

_____

_____

_____

_____

_____

_____

TODAY'S PERSONAL-EMPOWERMENT LEVEL:

Do stuff. Be clenched, curious. Not waiting
for inspiration's shove or society's kiss on
your forehead.

_____

SUSAN SONTAG

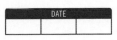

DATE		

HOW I'M MAKING MY VOICE HEARD TODAY:

_____

_____

_____

_____

_____

_____

_____

_____

_____

_____

_____

_____

_____

_____

_____

_____

_____

_____

_____

_____

_____

_____

_____

_____

TODAY'S PERSONAL-EMPOWERMENT LEVEL:

I will not have my life narrowed down. I will not bow down to somebody else's whim or to someone else's ignorance.

BELL HOOKS

HOW I'M MAKING MY VOICE HEARD TODAY:

TODAY'S PERSONAL-EMPOWERMENT LEVEL:

Every human body has its optimum weight and contour, which only health and efficiency can establish. Whenever we treat women's bodies as aesthetic objects without function we deform them.

GERMAINE GREER

DATE

HOW I'M MAKING MY VOICE HEARD TODAY:

_____
_____
_____
_____
_____
_____
_____
_____
_____
_____
_____
_____
_____
_____
_____
_____
_____
_____
_____
_____
_____
_____
_____
_____
_____

TODAY'S PERSONAL-EMPOWERMENT LEVEL:

One is not born, but rather becomes, a woman.

SIMONE DE BEAUVOIR

DATE	

HOW I'M MAKING MY VOICE HEARD TODAY:

TODAY'S PERSONAL-EMPOWERMENT LEVEL:

Women are leaders everywhere you look—
from the CEO who runs a Fortune 500
company to the housewife who raises
her children and heads her household.

NANCY PELOSI

HOW I'M MAKING MY VOICE HEARD TODAY:

_____

_____

_____

_____

_____

_____

_____

_____

_____

_____

_____

_____

_____

_____

_____

_____

_____

_____

_____

_____

_____

_____

_____

_____

_____

TODAY'S PERSONAL-EMPOWERMENT LEVEL:

It's just learning not to take the first no. And if you can't go straight ahead, you go around the corner.

CHER

DATE		

HOW I'M MAKING MY VOICE HEARD TODAY:

_____

_____

_____

_____

_____

_____

_____

_____

_____

_____

_____

_____

_____

_____

_____

_____

_____

_____

_____

_____

_____

_____

_____

TODAY'S PERSONAL-EMPOWERMENT LEVEL:

I'm not going anywhere. I'm going
to stay right here and cause all kinds
of trouble.

KATNISS *(THE HUNGER GAMES)*

HOW I'M MAKING MY VOICE HEARD TODAY:

_____

_____

_____

_____

_____

_____

_____

_____

_____

_____

_____

_____

_____

_____

_____

_____

_____

_____

_____

_____

_____

TODAY'S PERSONAL-EMPOWERMENT LEVEL:

I say if I'm beautiful. I say if I'm strong. You will not determine my story— I will.

AMY SCHUMER

HOW I'M MAKING MY VOICE HEARD TODAY:

TODAY'S PERSONAL-EMPOWERMENT LEVEL:

Beware of the man
who denounces
women writers;
his penis is tiny
& cannot spell.

ERICA JONG

HOW I'M MAKING MY VOICE HEARD TODAY:

_____

_____

_____

_____

_____

_____

_____

_____

_____

_____

_____

_____

_____

_____

_____

_____

_____

_____

_____

_____

_____

_____

_____

_____

TODAY'S PERSONAL-EMPOWERMENT LEVEL:

Yes, raising daughters more like our sons is a good thing. But how about raising our sons more like our daughters?

GLORIA STEINEM

DATE

HOW I'M MAKING MY VOICE HEARD TODAY:

_____
_____
_____
_____
_____
_____
_____
_____
_____
_____
_____
_____
_____
_____
_____
_____
_____
_____
_____
_____
_____
_____
_____
_____

TODAY'S PERSONAL-EMPOWERMENT LEVEL:

We need to understand that feminism is not for women, it's for humanity.

ANI DIFRANCO

HOW I'M MAKING MY VOICE HEARD TODAY:

_____
_____
_____
_____
_____
_____
_____
_____
_____
_____
_____
_____
_____
_____
_____
_____
_____
_____
_____
_____
_____
_____
_____

TODAY'S PERSONAL-EMPOWERMENT LEVEL:

When you work with the sort of really strong women that I work with, the idea that anyone would want to make decisions for them is hard to wrap your head around.

SETH MEYERS

DATE

HOW I'M MAKING MY VOICE HEARD TODAY:

_____

_____

_____

_____

_____

_____

_____

_____

_____

_____

_____

_____

_____

_____

_____

_____

_____

_____

_____

_____

_____

_____

_____

_____

TODAY'S PERSONAL-EMPOWERMENT LEVEL:

I believe any woman who is willing to struggle, strive—and if necessary learn karate—to make their mark in the world is a feminist.

MISS PIGGY

DATE		

HOW I'M MAKING MY VOICE HEARD TODAY:

_____

_____

_____

_____

_____

_____

_____

_____

_____

_____

_____

_____

_____

_____

_____

_____

_____

_____

_____

_____

_____

_____

_____

TODAY'S PERSONAL-EMPOWERMENT LEVEL:

No country can ever truly flourish if it stifles the potential of its women and deprives itself of the contributions of half of its citizens.

MICHELLE OBAMA

DATE		

HOW I'M MAKING MY VOICE HEARD TODAY:

_____

_____

_____

_____

_____

_____

_____

_____

_____

_____

_____

_____

_____

_____

_____

_____

_____

_____

_____

_____

_____

_____

_____

_____

TODAY'S PERSONAL-EMPOWERMENT LEVEL:

I finally got my answer to that question:
Who do you think you are?
I am whoever I say I am.

AMERICA FERRERA

DATE		

HOW I'M MAKING MY VOICE HEARD TODAY:

_____

_____

_____

_____

_____

_____

_____

_____

_____

_____

_____

_____

_____

_____

_____

_____

_____

_____

_____

_____

_____

TODAY'S PERSONAL-EMPOWERMENT LEVEL:

I don't believe there's a certain age where you can't say and feel and be who you want to be.

MADONNA

HOW I'M MAKING MY VOICE HEARD TODAY:

_____

_____

_____

_____

_____

_____

_____

_____

_____

_____

_____

_____

_____

_____

_____

_____

_____

_____

_____

_____

_____

_____

TODAY'S PERSONAL-EMPOWERMENT LEVEL:

Last time I checked, how much sex a girl
has doesn't justify a label slapped on her
like a soup can.

———————

MEGGIE ROYER

DATE

HOW I'M MAKING MY VOICE HEARD TODAY:

_____

_____

_____

_____

_____

_____

_____

_____

_____

_____

_____

_____

_____

_____

_____

_____

_____

_____

_____

_____

_____

TODAY'S PERSONAL-EMPOWERMENT LEVEL:

If you want to get something done, ask a woman.

MARGARET THATCHER

	DATE	

HOW I'M MAKING MY VOICE HEARD TODAY:

_____

_____

_____

_____

_____

_____

_____

_____

_____

_____

_____

_____

_____

_____

_____

_____

_____

_____

_____

_____

_____

_____

_____

_____

_____

_____

TODAY'S PERSONAL-EMPOWERMENT LEVEL:

There is no other organ quite like the uterus. If men had such an organ, they would brag about it. So should we.

INA MAY GASKIN

DATE

HOW I'M MAKING MY VOICE HEARD TODAY:

_____
_____
_____
_____
_____
_____
_____
_____
_____
_____
_____
_____
_____
_____
_____
_____
_____
_____
_____
_____
_____
_____
_____
_____

TODAY'S PERSONAL-EMPOWERMENT LEVEL:

Who run the world? Girls.

BEYONCÉ

DATE	

HOW I'M MAKING MY VOICE HEARD TODAY:

_____

_____

_____

_____

_____

_____

_____

_____

_____

_____

_____

_____

_____

_____

_____

_____

_____

_____

_____

_____

TODAY'S PERSONAL-EMPOWERMENT LEVEL:

We come here to stand shoulder to shoulder to make clear: We are here, we will not be silent, we will not play dead, we will fight for what we believe in.

ELIZABETH WARREN

DATE		

HOW I'M MAKING MY VOICE HEARD TODAY:

_____

_____

_____

_____

_____

_____

_____

_____

_____

_____

_____

_____

_____

_____

_____

_____

_____

_____

_____

_____

_____

_____

_____

TODAY'S PERSONAL-EMPOWERMENT LEVEL:

Courage to be is the key to the revelatory power of the feminist revolution.

MARY DALY

DATE

HOW I'M MAKING MY VOICE HEARD TODAY:

_____

_____

_____

_____

_____

_____

_____

_____

_____

_____

_____

_____

_____

_____

_____

_____

_____

_____

_____

_____

_____

_____

_____

TODAY'S PERSONAL-EMPOWERMENT LEVEL:

It's about being alive and feisty and not sitting down and shutting up even though people would like you to.

PINK

DATE		

HOW I'M MAKING MY VOICE HEARD TODAY:

_____

_____

_____

_____

_____

_____

_____

_____

_____

_____

_____

_____

_____

_____

_____

_____

_____

_____

_____

_____

_____

_____

_____

_____

TODAY'S PERSONAL-EMPOWERMENT LEVEL:

You may shoot me with your words,
You may cut me with your eyes,

You may kill me with your hatefulness,
But still, like air, I'll rise.

———

MAYA ANGELOU

HOW I'M MAKING MY VOICE HEARD TODAY:

_____

_____

_____

_____

_____

_____

_____

_____

_____

_____

_____

_____

_____

_____

_____

_____

_____

_____

_____

_____

_____

_____

_____

_____

TODAY'S PERSONAL-EMPOWERMENT LEVEL:

For us to have
self-esteem is truly
an act of revolution
and our revolution
is long overdue.

MARGARET CHO

HOW I'M MAKING MY VOICE HEARD TODAY:

_____

_____

_____

_____

_____

_____

_____

_____

_____

_____

_____

_____

_____

_____

_____

_____

_____

_____

_____

_____

_____

_____

_____

_____

_____

_____

TODAY'S PERSONAL-EMPOWERMENT LEVEL:

All men should be feminists. If men care about women's rights the world will be a better place.

———

JOHN LEGEND

HOW I'M MAKING MY VOICE HEARD TODAY:

_____

_____

_____

_____

_____

_____

_____

_____

_____

_____

_____

_____

_____

_____

_____

_____

_____

_____

_____

_____

_____

_____

TODAY'S PERSONAL-EMPOWERMENT LEVEL:

Women are the real architects of society.

HARRIET BEECHER STOWE

HOW I'M MAKING MY VOICE HEARD TODAY:

TODAY'S PERSONAL-EMPOWERMENT LEVEL:

A good woman
is one who loves
passionately, has
guts, seriousness and
passionate convictions,
takes responsibility,
and shapes society.

BETTY FRIEDAN

HOW I'M MAKING MY VOICE HEARD TODAY:

_____

_____

_____

_____

_____

_____

_____

_____

_____

_____

_____

_____

_____

_____

_____

_____

_____

_____

_____

_____

_____

_____

_____

TODAY'S PERSONAL-EMPOWERMENT LEVEL:

There is no such thing as a perfect feminist, and I am no exception.

LENA DUNHAM

HOW I'M MAKING MY VOICE HEARD TODAY:

_____

_____

_____

_____

_____

_____

_____

_____

_____

_____

_____

_____

_____

_____

_____

_____

_____

_____

_____

_____

_____

_____

TODAY'S PERSONAL-EMPOWERMENT LEVEL:

The success of every woman should be the inspiration to another. We should raise each other up.

SERENA WILLIAMS

HOW I'M MAKING MY VOICE HEARD TODAY:

_____

_____

_____

_____

_____

_____

_____

_____

_____

_____

_____

_____

_____

_____

_____

_____

_____

_____

_____

_____

_____

_____

_____

TODAY'S PERSONAL-EMPOWERMENT LEVEL:

People ask me sometimes, when— when do you think it will it be enough? When will there be enough women on the court? And my answer is when there are nine.

RUTH BADER GINSBURG

DATE

HOW I'M MAKING MY VOICE HEARD TODAY:

_____

_____

_____

_____

_____

_____

_____

_____

_____

_____

_____

_____

_____

_____

_____

_____

_____

_____

_____

_____

_____

_____

_____

_____

TODAY'S PERSONAL-EMPOWERMENT LEVEL:

We could eradicate polio. I don't see
why we can't eradicate misogyny.

_____

ALAN ALDA

HOW I'M MAKING MY VOICE HEARD TODAY:

_____

_____

_____

_____

_____

_____

_____

_____

_____

_____

_____

_____

_____

_____

_____

_____

_____

_____

_____

_____

_____

_____

_____

_____

_____

_____

TODAY'S PERSONAL-EMPOWERMENT LEVEL:

I'm not ashamed to dress "like a woman" because I don't think it's shameful to be a woman.

IGGY POP

DATE	

HOW I'M MAKING MY VOICE HEARD TODAY:

_____
_____
_____
_____
_____
_____
_____
_____
_____
_____
_____
_____
_____
_____
_____
_____
_____
_____
_____
_____
_____
_____
_____
_____

TODAY'S PERSONAL-EMPOWERMENT LEVEL:

It is time that we all see gender as a spectrum instead of two sets of opposing ideals. We should stop defining each other by what we are not and start defining ourselves by who we are.

EMMA WATSON

HOW I'M MAKING MY VOICE HEARD TODAY:

TODAY'S PERSONAL-EMPOWERMENT LEVEL:

Wonder Woman is a state of mind.

WRDSMTH

DATE

HOW I'M MAKING MY VOICE HEARD TODAY:

_____
_____
_____
_____
_____
_____
_____
_____
_____
_____
_____
_____
_____
_____
_____
_____
_____
_____
_____
_____
_____

TODAY'S PERSONAL-EMPOWERMENT LEVEL:

Every day, I define myself. I know who I am today. I don't promise you anything for tomorrow.

———

SALMA HAYEK

HOW I'M MAKING MY VOICE HEARD TODAY:

_____

_____

_____

_____

_____

_____

_____

_____

_____

_____

_____

_____

_____

_____

_____

_____

_____

_____

_____

_____

_____

_____

_____

TODAY'S PERSONAL-EMPOWERMENT LEVEL:

I'd rather take coffee
than compliments
just now.

——————

LOUISA MAY ALCOTT

HOW I'M MAKING MY VOICE HEARD TODAY:

_____

_____

_____

_____

_____

_____

_____

_____

_____

_____

_____

_____

_____

_____

_____

_____

_____

_____

_____

_____

_____

_____

_____

_____

TODAY'S PERSONAL-EMPOWERMENT LEVEL:

"Are you trying to have it all?" That question makes no sense. It's a stupid question. Stop asking it.

LESLIE KNOPE *(PARKS AND RECREATION)*

	DATE	

HOW I'M MAKING MY VOICE HEARD TODAY:

_____

_____

_____

_____

_____

_____

_____

_____

_____

_____

_____

_____

_____

_____

_____

_____

_____

_____

_____

_____

_____

_____

_____

_____

_____

TODAY'S PERSONAL-EMPOWERMENT LEVEL:

It's not about being more powerful than men—it's about having equal rights with protection, support, justice. It's about very basic things. It's not a badge like a fashion item.

ANNIE LENNOX

HOW I'M MAKING MY VOICE HEARD TODAY:

_____

_____

_____

_____

_____

_____

_____

_____

_____

_____

_____

_____

_____

_____

_____

_____

_____

_____

_____

_____

_____

_____

_____

_____

TODAY'S PERSONAL-EMPOWERMENT LEVEL:

Feminism is not just the belief that men and women are equal. It's the knowledge that when we are all equal, all of us are more free.

JUSTIN TRUDEAU

DATE		

HOW I'M MAKING MY VOICE HEARD TODAY:

_____

_____

_____

_____

_____

_____

_____

_____

_____

_____

_____

_____

_____

_____

_____

_____

_____

_____

_____

_____

_____

_____

_____

_____

_____

TODAY'S PERSONAL-EMPOWERMENT LEVEL:

We no longer live in the blank white spaces at the edge of print. We no longer live in the gaps between the stories. We are the story in print. And we are writing the story ourselves.

ELISABETH MOSS

HOW I'M MAKING MY VOICE HEARD TODAY:

_____

_____

_____

_____

_____

_____

_____

_____

_____

_____

_____

_____

_____

_____

_____

_____

_____

_____

_____

_____

_____

_____

_____

_____

_____

_____

TODAY'S PERSONAL-EMPOWERMENT LEVEL:

People can tell you to keep your mouth shut, but it doesn't stop you from having your own opinion!

ANNE FRANK

HOW I'M MAKING MY VOICE HEARD TODAY:

_____

_____

_____

_____

_____

_____

_____

_____

_____

_____

_____

_____

_____

_____

_____

_____

_____

_____

_____

_____

_____

_____

_____

TODAY'S PERSONAL-EMPOWERMENT LEVEL:

You want a revolution? I want a revelation

So listen to my declaration:

"We hold these truths to be self-evident
  That all men are created equal"

And when I meet Thomas Jefferson

I'm 'a compel him to include women
  in the sequel!

———————————

ANGELICA SCHUYLER *(HAMILTON)*

HOW I'M MAKING MY VOICE HEARD TODAY:

_____

_____

_____

_____

_____

_____

_____

_____

_____

_____

_____

_____

_____

_____

_____

_____

_____

_____

_____

_____

_____

_____

TODAY'S PERSONAL-EMPOWERMENT LEVEL:

Women are not the weak, frail little flowers that they are advertised.

WILL ROGERS

DATE		

HOW I'M MAKING MY VOICE HEARD TODAY:

_____

_____

_____

_____

_____

_____

_____

_____

_____

_____

_____

_____

_____

_____

_____

_____

_____

_____

_____

_____

_____

_____

TODAY'S PERSONAL-EMPOWERMENT LEVEL:

After all those years as a woman hearing "not thin enough, not pretty enough, not smart enough, not this enough, not that enough," almost overnight I woke up one morning and thought, "I'm enough."

ANNA QUINDLEN

DATE		

HOW I'M MAKING MY VOICE HEARD TODAY:

_____

_____

_____

_____

_____

_____

_____

_____

_____

_____

_____

_____

_____

_____

_____

_____

_____

_____

_____

_____

_____

_____

_____

_____

TODAY'S PERSONAL-EMPOWERMENT LEVEL:

If you retain nothing else, always remember the most important Rule of Beauty. "Who cares?"

TINA FEY

DATE		

HOW I'M MAKING MY VOICE HEARD TODAY:

_____

_____

_____

_____

_____

_____

_____

_____

_____

_____

_____

_____

_____

_____

_____

_____

_____

_____

_____

_____

_____

_____

_____

_____

_____

_____

TODAY'S PERSONAL-EMPOWERMENT LEVEL:

Human rights are women's rights and women's rights are human rights, once and for all.

HILLARY CLINTON

DATE

HOW I'M MAKING MY VOICE HEARD TODAY:

_____
_____
_____
_____
_____
_____
_____
_____
_____
_____
_____
_____
_____
_____
_____
_____
_____
_____
_____
_____
_____
_____

TODAY'S PERSONAL-EMPOWERMENT LEVEL:

Rock on, sister.

(Or brother, or whatever!)

————

KNOCK KNOCK